more than the score…

ROBERT SCHUMANN

'Reverie' from

Scenes from Childhood

for piano solo

Presented by Daniel Grimwood

Contents

Daniel Grimwood talks about
Schumann's 'Reverie'. 2

'Reverie' 4

About the composer. 6

About the music 6

This publication draws on material released by
Edition Peters in the *Piano Masterworks* collection on
Tido Music, a revolutionary web resource and iPad app.

PETERS EDITION LTD

A member of the EDITION PETERS GROUP
LEIPZIG · LONDON · NEW YORK

Published by Peters Edition Ltd, London
2–6 Baches Street   London N1 6DN
www.editionpeters.com
This edition © 2017 by Peters Edition Ltd, London

Daniel Grimwood

talks about

Schumann's 'Reverie'

Schumann's piano music represents the pinnacle of German Romanticism. In this work, *Kinderszenen (Scenes from Childhood)*, he was writing music thinking about his own children, and parenthood, I suspect. And although these pieces come under the guise of music written for children to play, this is very much music for grown-ups.

Schumann's musical personality is embodied by two characters he created: Eusebius and Florestan – one dreamy and the other vigorous. These two characters appeared as a result of Schumann's journalistic endeavours: when he was talking about works by other composers he would imagine conversations between these two characters who represented different versions of himself. They later started to appear in his piano works, and it can be said that they appear in all his music.

Kinderszenen is a collection of miniatures that can be performed as a cycle, though many of them work beautifully as free-standing pieces. The structure of the *Kinderszenen* is really rather wonderful and quite interesting because the title is already suggestive – 'Scenes from Childhood' is not the same as saying music that's written for children. Children can play most of it, it's true, but it's more to do with the nature of childhood and its relationship to adulthood. In the first piece, 'Of foreign lands', and how it relates to the final piece, 'The Poet Speaks' – who narrates it? Is it narrated by the child, or is it narrated by the poet? Do they interact with each other? In 'Träumerei' ('Dreaming'), who is doing the dreaming? The child is definitely falling asleep: it seems to me that the poet presents the cycle in the first piece by imagining the child; the child falls asleep and dreams of the poet. And so it goes full circle, playing on the idea that all children yearn to be adults, and all adults yearn to recapture what they lost when their childhood ended.

In 'Träumerei', the person who dreams may or may not be asleep: we don't know whether this is music of sleep or of daydreaming. And the arch of the melody itself seems to suggest you can imagine somebody rolling their eyes and looking at imagined figures.

Metre and metronome marks

Schumann deliberately blurs the metre by having displaced accents: a melody that starts without any accompanying notes on an anacrusis, a harmony chord that comes in on a second beat, and you have to get some way into the piece before you actually understand, as the listener, where the main beats are. It's only really on the final cadence where you understand that that's the first beat.

> *Clara said: 'Please ignore my husband's metronome markings: they're rubbish'*

There's a controversy about Schumann's metronome marks in this music, and about his metronome marks in general. His wife Clara said, 'Please ignore my husband's metronome markings: they're rubbish,' or something to that effect. So clearly in her own edition of his music she changed many of the metronome markings and made them more realistic. Or did she?

We know that the Schumanns owned a Conrad Graf fortepiano: these instruments were still in use when the Érards had started building much more sonorous pianos. The faster tempi certainly worked better on the older pianos, so maybe his rather extreme crotchet = 100 metronome marking in this work makes sense when played on the older pianos. I've tried playing it on a modern piano at that metronome mark and it just feels very hurried. That said, it could signify to us that this isn't intended to be a slow movement. Maybe that tells us more – maybe this tells us this is music of day-dreaming rather than sleep-dreaming.

Phrases and phrasing

In terms of achieving a nicely balanced chord in the first bar, Schumann does the work for us (as he so often does) by overlapping the hands – the thumbs overlap – which gives you a very natural sonority focused on the internal third. Having a chord voiced in the middle creates a warmth and a glow to the sound.

It's important that we closely observe the slurs in this music and consider what they tell us about the melody. If you look at the music, you'll notice that we have short slur lengths, whereas from bar 6 we have one long phrase. With the shorter phrases, you'll also notice that they go up at the end, so they're like small questions. They should be separated. But this time, let it move forwards more. It's very important that, at the top of these arches, the melody note isn't lost in order to accommodate the grace notes in the left hand.

In bar 3 there's a rather beautiful small *crescendo* hairpin marked in the left hand, and these intervals are horn calls. Horn calls in German Romanticism have associations with hunting, and the hunt in German Romanticism has an association with memory and recollection, so it's a little moment of recollection in the centre of the phrase.

In bar 7, as the melody falls down, the inner voices follow suit and they seem to call to each other and answer: all the other voices move in sympathy with the melody voice and help it on its way back to the repeat mark.

Each time the melody returns, the upbeat is written differently, so in the beginning we have a single voice. At the repeat marking we have an eighth note. In bar 17 we have a grace note and in bar 20 we have two voices playing the same note suggesting that it needs to have a little more emphasis.

To my mind the climax of this short piece arrives three bars before the end, where both of the hands have to be stretched out in a gesture of appeasement. This is the moment of absolute magic which crowns this piece.

Pedalling

Schumann said that he always began a piece of music with the pedal down, and he will right-pedal fairly uniformly at the beginning of many movements in his works. Obviously, this does not mean that the pedal should be held down throughout but it means that it should be used liberally.

> *It's important that we closely observe the slurs in this music and what they tell us about the melody*

Ritardandi and flexibility of tempo

One trait of Schumann is to write *ritardandi* without actually notating where one should pick the tempo up again, so a great deal is left to the discretion of the performer. There are so many different ways of dealing with this and I think Schumann was an improviser and there should be this freshly dreamt-up quality to a lot of his music, that nothing should sound too planned. Indeed, I go so far as to say

that nothing should be too planned. We should never start playing it knowing exactly how it's going to turn out. Thinking about the *ritardando* at the end, it doesn't necessarily mean that we have to slow down all the way to the final beat. Again, we have short phrases

Schumann's Kinderszenen *inspired many other musical depictions of childhood.*

with the question marks at the end where the melody sort of lilts upwards. So it can be quite nice to actually finish the piece picking up the tempo in the last three notes rather than slowing it down all the way to the end. Equally, we can slow it down all the way to the end and it can still be beautiful.

Flexibility of tempo in much of Schumann's music is of paramount importance, and not least of all because he was an improviser, and improvisers tend not to think in terms of barlines. He does tell us a great deal about what we can do with the tempo. He marks in these *ritardandi*; he doesn't tell us where to finish them. He gives us phrase marks of varying lengths and, if one obeys them, with the shorter phrases with the little question marks on the end. They take time. It suggests that we can have these little lilting gaps between the phrases, or the cascading falling phrases which can move on a little bit more.

In my opinion, the tempo for this movement should be in constant flux. We want to soften the contours as far as possible. Schumann's already given us enough pointers that this is where he's driving at anyway, so we can take it one step further by going with the ebb and flow where it feels natural to do so.

Daniel Grimwood is a performer of international renown, and has performed a wide variety of music in prestigious venues in London, New York, Moscow, and across Europe, North America, Asia and Africa

'Reverie'

from *Scenes from Childhood*

Robert Schumann (1810–1856)

ritard.

Edition Peters 73161

Based on EP 9500b, edited by Hans Joachim Köhler

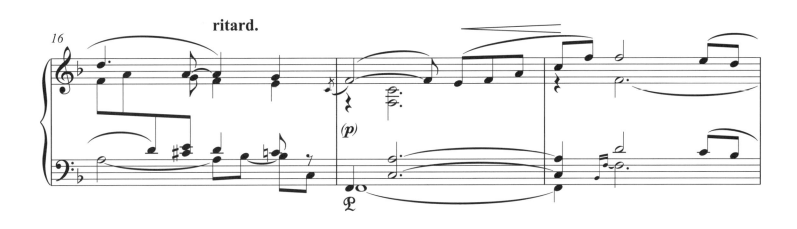

About Robert Schumann...

Robert Schumann was born on 8 June 1810 in Zwickau. As a child, Schumann studied piano with a local organist. His first compositions date from the early 1820s, and his first songs and writings from 1827.

Schumann's literary, philosophical and musical tendencies increasingly came to take priority over his later law studies. By 1830 he had committed himself to becoming a concert pianist. Paralysis in his right hand curtailed these hopes in 1832, and at this point he began composing in earnest, including many of his major piano works, including *Carnaval* and *Kinderszenen*. In 1835 Schumann also became the editor of the *Neue Zeitschrift für Musik*.

In 1844 Schumann's health began to show signs of failing. He gave up the editorship of the *Neue Zeitschrift für Musik*. Freed from the responsibilities of literary editorship, composition flourished.

From 1852, however, his health problems became serious. In February 1854 he attempted suicide and was admitted to an asylum in Endenich, where he died two and a half years later, on 29 July 1856.

Emily Kilpatrick

Robert Schumann

Clara Wieck

Kinderszenen...

Schumann's *Kinderszenen* was composed in 1838, during the period of his engagement to Clara Wieck. One of the touchstones of the nineteenth-century musical imagination, it became the reference standard for subsequent musical depictions of childhood. *Kinderszenen* is inextricably bound to the Romantic aesthetic: for a composer saturated in the writings of Jean Paul and his disciples, childhood symbolised purity and intrinsic truth, and profundity of meaning was best achieved through simplicity of expression.

While the pieces' straightforward lyricism and strophic forms evoke a childlike concentration of mood, the composer underlined that they were intended as 'reflections by an adult, for adults'. He also explained that the titles had largely been determined after the pieces had been composed, 'as delicate hints for performance and interpretation'. The final movement, 'Der Dichter spricht' ('The poet speaks') retrospectively confirms this: 'the poet' is present throughout, watching, commenting, imagining and remembering.

Emily Kilpatrick

Transform your piano playing

Tido Music is a revolutionary web resource for the discovery, study and performance of piano music.

Enjoy unlimited access to a growing library of sheet music online, brought to life with recordings, video performances and more.

Whether you're a student, a teacher or an advanced pianist, Tido will guide and inspire you.

Piano Masterworks, the first collection to appear on the platform, launched with content from Edition Peters.

Enhance your experience with Tido Music for iPad

- The app listens to you play and turns pages automatically!
- Leading pianists share insight on technique and interpretation in video masterclasses

Piano Masterworks

The rapidly expanding *Piano Masterworks* collection includes the following titles from Edition Peters:

Albéniz, I.	España Op. 165
Bach, J. S.	15 Two-part Inventions; French Suite No. 5; Goldberg Variations; The Well-tempered Clavier, Book 1; The Well-tempered Clavier, Book 2; 15 Three-part Inventions (Sinfonias); Partita No. 4 in D major; Toccata in D minor; Italian Concerto
Bach, C. P. E.	Solfeggio H220
Beethoven, L. van	Bagatelles; Für Elise; Sonata 'Pathétique' in C minor; Sonata in G major Op. 49 No. 2; 'Moonlight' Sonata in C sharp minor; Sonata in F minor Op. 2 No. 1; 'The Tempest' Sonata in D minor; 6 Variations in F major
Brahms, J.	4 Piano Pieces Op. 119; 6 Piano Pieces Op. 118; 3 Intermezzi Op. 117
Cage, J.	A Room; Dream; In a Landscape; Opening Dance for Sue Laub; Suite for Toy Piano; Three Easy Pieces
Chopin, F.	Waltz in C sharp minor Op. 64 No. 2; 24 Préludes Op. 28
Clementi, M.	Sonatinas Op. 36
Debussy, C.	Deux Arabesques; Children's Corner; La Cathédrale Engloutie; Suite Bergamasque
Fauré, G.	Pavane Op. 50; Pièces Brèves Op. 84
Field, J.	Nocturnes
Grieg, E.	Holberg Suite Op. 40; Lyric Pieces Book 1; Lyric Pieces Book 2
Handel, G. F.	Suite No. 5 in E Major 'The Harmonious Blacksmith'
Haydn, J.	Sonata in D major Hob. XVI:37
Janáček, L.	On an Overgrown Path
Liszt, F.	Consolations; Liebesträume; 2 Pieces from Weihnachtsbaum
Mendelssohn, F.	Songs Without Words Book 1; Songs Without Words Book 6
Mozart, W. A.	Adagio for Glass Harmonica; Adagio in B minor; Fantasy in D minor; Sonata in C major; Sonata in A minor
Musorgsky, M.	Pictures from an Exhibition
Ravel, M.	À la Manière de Chabrier; Pavane pour une Infante défunte
Satie, E.	3 Gnossiennes; 3 Gymnopédies
Schubert, F.	Impromptu in E flat major; Impromptu in G flat major; 6 Moments Musicaux
Scriabin, A.	Etude in C sharp minor; Prelude in C sharp minor (for Left Hand)
Scarlatti, D.	Sonata in E major K162
Schumann, R.	Album for the Young; Scenes from Childhood; Waldszenen
Tchaikovsky, P. I.	The Seasons; Album for the Young